HOW TO GET THE MOST OUT OF

SUGGESTIONS FOR GROUP LEADERS

We're deliberately not prescriptive, and differer   s, but here are a few tried-and-trusted ideas ...

1. THE ROOM Encourage people to sit within t

2. HOSPITALITY Tea or coffee and biscuits on a   ....uiiy is always appreciated and encourages people to talk infor.   , .

3. THE START If group members don't know one another well, some kind of 'icebreaker' might be helpful. Be careful to place a time limit on this exercise!

4. PREPARING THE GROUP Explain that there are no right or wrong answers, and that among friends it is fine to say things that you're not sure about – to express half-formed ideas. If individuals choose to say nothing, that's all right too.

5. THE MATERIAL It helps if each group member has their own personal copy of this course book. Encourage members to read each session *before* the meeting. There's no need to consider all the questions. A lively exchange of views is what matters, so be selective. The quotations in blue are there to stimulate discussion and – just like the opinions expressed by the audio participants – don't necessarily represent York Courses' views or beliefs.

6. PREPARATION It's not compulsory for group members to have a Bible, but it might be helpful for at least the leader to have one handy. Ask in advance if you want anyone to lead prayers or read aloud, so they can prepare.

7. TIMING Aim to start on time and stick fairly closely to your stated finishing time.

8. USING THE AUDIO/VIDEO For each of the sessions, we recommend reading through the session in the course booklet before listening together to the corresponding session on the audio material/watching the video. Groups may like to choose a question to discuss straight after they have listened to/watched a relevant track on the audio/video – but there are no hard-and-fast rules. Do whatever works best for your group!

9. THE TRANSCRIPT Included at the end of the course booklet, the transcript is a written record of the audio/video material and will be invaluable as you prepare.

RUNNING A VIRTUAL HOUSE GROUP AND SHARING AUDIO/VIDEO

To run your virtual group, use software such as Zoom or Google Meet, and use the 'Share Screen' function to share the audio/video with your group.

HOW TO DOWNLOAD THE AUDIO AND VIDEO

To access the downloadable videos that come with the course book, go to https://spckpublishing.co.uk/who-am-I-video You can watch and download the videos there. To download the audio, go to https://spckpublishing.co.uk/who-am-I-york-courses audio/ and use the code WhoAmIMP3 to purchase the audio for free on the site.

The full list of available formats is as follows:

- Course book, including transcript of video and access to video/audio downloads (paperback 978-1-91584-354-8)
- Course book, including transcript of video and access to video/audio downloads (eBook 978-1-91584-357-9, both ePub and Mobi files provided)
- Participants' book, including transcript of video: pack of 5 (paperback 978-1-91584-355-5)
- Participants' book, including transcript of video (eBook 978-1-91584-356-2, both ePub and Mobi files provided)
- Video of discussion to support *Who Am I?*, available via the course book with access to audio and video downloads
- Audio book of discussion to support *Who Am I?* (audio/digital download)

WHO AM I?

An ecumenical course in four sessions

Nick Baines

spck

YORK
COURSES

CONTENTS

Sessions

Transcript

SESSION 1
WHO AM I?

At the beginning of the biblical story we find Adam and Eve in a garden. They manage to mess up with the first thing that tempts them and they respond predictably: they run and hide, hoping no one will notice. Surprisingly, it is God who comes looking for them. Then God poses the question every human being faces at some point: 'You mortal human being, where are you?'

'We're children of God through our blood kinship with Christ. We're also sons and daughters of Adam and Eve, with a hereditary craving for forbidden fruit salad.'[1].
BARBARA BROWN TAYLOR

This question hides another fundamental question: 'Who do you think you are?' And the answers to these questions are, in one sense, what the biblical writers spend the next fifteen hundred years wrestling with. Who are we? Where are we in relation to God, each other and the 'garden'? Why, in the end, do we matter? The answers aren't obvious at first glance – nor should they be assumed or merely taken for granted. But the answers we own in the end will have far-reaching consequences for the way we live, the priorities we set in life, the morality we espouse and the value we put on relationships, things, values and behaviour.

'The mystery of human existence lies not in just staying alive, but in finding something to live for.'[2]
FYODOR DOSTOEVSKY

Yet even in these few verses in Genesis 3, we catch a glimpse of where to begin. We don't find God; we discover that God has already come looking for and found us. God is not surprised that we instinctively hide from him. These questions assume human mortality – and the implicit acknowledgement that human beings have to answer them knowing that one day they will die. God knows we are human.

'We may ignore, but we can nowhere evade the presence of God. The world is crowded with Him. He walks everywhere incognito.'[3]
C. S. LEWIS

How would we have answered God's question in the garden?

Well, I think it might be worth starting by considering the world we live in today and some of the complexities thrown up by how the world now is. At the time of writing, the world of God's good creation is wracked by war, mass displacement of people, gross pollution of our essential water sources, wilful avoidance of facing up to the costs of global warming, and the development of technology. In fact, this last point sounds almost banal until we factor in the scandal that while millions of people – made in God's image? – suffer primitive conditions and avoidable suffering and alienation, a few others make more money than whole countries might need for their people to survive (let alone thrive). And then there is artificial intelligence (AI), which is revolutionising the world in the areas of knowledge, communications, science, industry, education, business, religion and so on.

'[E]very human life is a reflection of divinity and, every act of injustice mars and defaces the image of God in man.'[4]
MARTIN LUTHER KING, JR

'Is the rich world aware of how four billion of the six billion live? If we were aware, we would want to help out, we'd want to get involved.'[5]
BILL GATES

It is challenges like these that drive many people to run and hide. They are too complicated, and we feel our limitations and failures too acutely. But face them we must if we are to be brave and realistic enough to address the questions. Let's have a brief look at some of them as we begin to clear the ground for some fresh thinking.

CLIMATE CHANGE

Even though some people question what is causing climate change, almost no one doubts it is happening. Experts might be derided by some politicians when they say something unpopular, but they are usually just drawing conclusions from evidence and presenting us with reality. Younger generations tend to be very motivated about global warming and its consequences, as they have their future ahead of them and expect to pass on something to their own children and grandchildren. But if we believe that 'the earth is the LORD's, and everything in it' (Psalm 24:1), how should we be responding to the eco-crisis – and those most affected by it? This raises questions about human responsibility and accountability, how we make our ethical judgements, and whether we truly believe that all people are made in the image of God.

'How could I look my grandchildren in the eye and say I knew what was happening to the world and did nothing?'[6]
DAVID ATTENBOROUGH

'We are each called to go through life reclaiming the planet an inch at a time until the Garden of Eden grows green again.'[7]
JOAN D. CHITTISTER

MIGRATION

In June 2024 I visited Sudan (against government advice). My diocese has had a strong link with the church in Sudan for over forty years, and we needed to be with our sisters and brothers in their distress. Sudan is riven by a civil war that has seen thousands brutally killed, thousands more sorely oppressed and over 11 million displaced. It is the world's worst conflict, yet it barely hits the media or political radar. It is estimated that around 350 million people around the planet are now migrants – most for reasons of survival, not economic tourism. Do these people matter? Is their suffering more than a social inconvenience?

'There's just no more compelling a story, no more compelling an issue, no more compelling a locus of human suffering than Sudan.'[8]
ERIC REEVES

'We can't deter people fleeing for their lives. They will come. The choice we have is how well we manage their arrival, and how humanely.'[9]
ANTONIO GUTERRES

CONFLICT

The consensus that has held the world in a relatively secure institutional place for eighty years since the Second World War has begun to fall apart in recent years. War on European soil was largely unthinkable – that was the whole point of the United Nations, the European Union and international courts of justice and human rights. And then came Ukraine, Gaza, Sudan, Yemen and so on. In the Second World War fifty million people – all sons and daughters, parents and friends – lost their lives in a battle for freedom, peace and power. Did those lives matter at all? Or only the ones fighting on 'the right side'?

'One is left with the horrible feeling now that war settles nothing; that to win a war is as disastrous as to lose one.'[10]
AGATHA CHRISTIE

TECHNOLOGY

In a single short lifetime the world has been revolutionised by technology. Getting our heads around hardware and software developments in the last twenty years has been tough enough, but the rapid advent of AI is throwing up massive opportunities and challenges for humanity. Although it has always been possible (and right) to say that technology depends on people, this is now, for the first time in history, looking a little naive. According to some of those at the forefront of AI exploration, we are now in a position where human agency or control is superseded by software that develops its own independent agency and has the potential to overrule human decision-making. So, what does it mean to be human if human beings become commodities for autonomous artificial agents whose fast decision-making makes humans redundant? Does being human ultimately matter any more?

'In this century, not only has science changed the world faster than ever, but in new and different ways. Targeted drugs, genetic modification, artificial intelligence, perhaps even implants into our brains – may change human beings themselves.'[11]
MARTIN REES

If all of the above has given you a headache and you fancy a break, then you are normal and can relax. These are not easy questions to address, but they cannot be ducked unless we want to abdicate human responsibility and leave it to others to shape our future for us – possibly according to beliefs or world views that aren't always noble.

'Let's show up to life. Let's prove how beautiful it can really be. Let's face the conflict, redeem it, conquer it, and allow it to mold our character. Let's participate in what God is doing in the world.'[12]
DONALD MILLER

The other thing to notice at this point is that the few challenges cited above (and there are many others we could have chosen) are all inextricably intertwined. The material resources that go into advanced technology are often rare, so owning their sources is a matter of economic and political significance. The drive for rare metals and minerals fuels conflict and power battles. In turn, these conflicts drive people out of their homes and countries, often starving them along the way, powering mass migration. Migration raises the political temperature of 'host' countries and leads to the hardening of attitudes towards minorities and 'others'. Further conflicts ensue and the 'never again' cry of previous suffering generations gets forgotten amid the clamour for power and security today.

Underlying this brief survey of contemporary human challenges (and opportunities, as AI might offer solutions to some thus far intractable global problems) lie these haunting questions. In the light of all this, what does it mean to be a human being? Are we just economic cogs in an out-of-control political game? Are we commodities to be traded on a market that dehumanises people, categorising them in order to remove their faces and voices? If this world is all there is, then why do I matter anyway?

Let me give a vivid, but possibly tendentious, example of why the question matters.

If you visit the Holocaust memorial museum of Yad Vashem in Jerusalem, you must find the specific memorial to the Warsaw ghetto. Rather than a single plinth or statue, there are two. One is a young man with a rifle leading the violent uprising, which says, 'We will not just sit here and suffer without a fight for our dignity.' The other side has a group of Jews, bowed down, walking like lambs to the slaughter, driven by Nazi soldiers ... who have no faces under their distinctive helmets. I once asked an academic there why the sculptor had made the Germans faceless. He replied to the effect that you cannot give a human face to this appalling evil. Is he right? Or should the Germans have been given faces in order to make it clear that it was human beings – like you and me – who dehumanised others so they could more easily dispose of them as if they were just inconvenient things? The question is not for me to resolve; it is for me to live within the tension of these two responses to unjust and systematic cruelty.

'The concentration camp is the final expression of human separateness and its ultimate consequence. It is organized abandonment.'[13]
ARTHUR MILLER

'In any kind of conflict, you have a certain dehumanization that comes along with it. And it's important as a reporter, a writer, a journalist, to try to restore humanity.'[14]
ANTHONY SHADID

So by now it will be clear that behind the decisions we make every day about all sorts of mundane things there lurk some haunting and vital choices. What is a human being? What is a human being worth? Are some human beings more valuable than others? How do we know? Are we actually being human if we give up human agency and responsibility to machines that can do things faster than we can? Is there such a thing as accountability, and if so, to whom and on what grounds?

None of this is new. The writers of the Scriptures wrestled with these fundamental questions. Scientists engage – often heroically – with fundamental matters of material importance (what is the universe?, how does it work?, why does it work? and so on), leading the rest of us to then do the hard work of asking the 'why' questions about meaning and significance. And this is the stuff of religion. For our part, Christian faith is not just about individual security for eternity, or worship of a tribal deity who, we hope, will defeat all the miseries of this world and help us eventually to escape them. No, Christian faith plunges us right into the heart of these material and spiritual questions. It is the whole reason we celebrate Christmas and God's opting to come among us as one of us, subject to all that it means to be human in a contingent world. Matter matters. The kingdom of God is no remote and disembodied fantasy land.

'The Almighty appeared on earth as a helpless human baby, needing to be fed and changed and taught to talk like any other child. The more you think about it, the more staggering it gets. Nothing in fiction is so fantastic as this truth of the Incarnation.'[15]
J. I. PACKER

CONCLUSION

Having identified some of the questions we face as we look towards Christmas and seek to re-shape the lens behind our tired eyes, we can now move on in the next session to ask what we find in the Bible that helps us address, as simply as possible, this fundamental conundrum: who am I and why do I matter? Or, should that be: who are we and why do we matter?

FOR DISCUSSION

1. Are the questions raised in this session the right ones for us to be asking in Advent?

2. How might I go about opening up these questions to my friends who might not share my particular faith?

3. Does my church make space for asking the questions behind the questions, allowing people to start from where they are in understanding what it is to be human and why our answer matters?

4. What do we find frightening about the future, and what might offer encouragement?

5. What does our theology do at this point to help us address basic human questions of meaning?

SESSION 2
WHAT DOES THE BIBLE SAY?

'What are human beings?' (Psalm 8:4). Indeed.

According to one nineteenth-century doctor, a kiss can be defined as 'the anatomical juxtaposition of two orbicularis oris muscles in a state of contraction'. Anyone who has done any kissing might think of it in somewhat different terms.

'How did it happen that their lips came together? How does it happen that birds sing, that snow melts, that the rose unfolds, that the dawn whitens behind the stark shapes of trees on the quivering summit of the hill? A kiss, and all was said.'[1]
VICTOR HUGO

Similarly, while being scientifically accurate, those who teach us that the human body is made up of around sixty chemical elements, might not be telling the whole story. If a human person is more than – rather than just or less than – a set of chemicals and physical attributes, why do we think this matters, and how might we describe it?

Well, anyone who seeks to offer an account of what it means to be human must begin not only with some 'stuff', but also with a set of assumptions. It might be a bit of an over-simplistic cliché, but the relationship between 'how' questions (the stuff of science) and 'why' questions (the stuff of religion and philosophy) is not straightforward.

And one fundamental is that (as the German philosopher Immanuel Kant suggested) implicit meaning cannot be derived automatically from mere existence.

So thinking about meaning and being requires us to make some assumptions of our own regarding what makes humanness distinct and meaningful. What makes an expression of love and affection more than 'the anatomical juxtaposition of two orbicularis'?

'I'm human, you're human, let me greet your humanness.
Let's be people together for a while.'[2]
ANNE LAMOTT

Christians address this question by referring to a narrative, not a scientific thesis. The Judeo-Christian tradition goes back between 3,000 and 4,000 years to a pre-scientific world. What we now call the Bible is a literary compendium of fifteen hundred years of reflection on just this question: what does it mean to be me and us? Through different times and places, diverse cultures and conditions, we read the developing stories and ruminations of real people and communities as they tried to make sense of life, history, morality, values, behaviour and mortality. Therefore, we shouldn't be surprised that this narrative offers a range of responses in a variety of languages – and they all struggle with the limitations and paradoxes of understanding.

'Many people think of the Bible as a book of moral teachings with stories sprinkled through to illustrate the teachings. But it's a lot BETTER THAN THAT ... the Bible is a single true story with teachings sprinkled through to illustrate the story.'[3]
TIMOTHY KELLER

'The book to read is not the one which thinks for you, but the one which makes you think. No book in the world equals the Bible for that.'[4]
DR JAMES McCOSH

Of course, the significant element of this developing narrative is that these human beings wrestle not only with life on earth, but with God, eternity and what it means to live right. The writers, no doubt distilling what were common questions in their particular cultures, cannot be satisfied with a formula that simply says that what is just is or what will be will be. So it might be useful to look at just some of the ways the Scriptures address what it might mean to be a human being.

GENESIS

The creation narratives (chapters 1 and 2), and what follows up to the end of what we have as chapter 11, set out a bold and audacious account of human beings living in community. Its starting point is that we are created out of self-giving love and, as created beings, are *mortal*. The fundamental fact of being alive is that we shall one day die. People should live their life in the light of this fact – and coming to terms with our mortality is, I suggest, the key to living a life of freedom, liberated from fear of death.

'Somebody should tell us, right at the start of our lives, that we are dying. Then we might live life to the limit, every minute of every day. Do it! I say. Whatever you want to do, do it now! There are only so many tomorrows.'[5]
MICHAEL LANDON

Acknowledgement of mortality assumes *moral accountability*. That is to say that if the fact of our eventual death suggests that *how* we now live matters, then morality (a framework for judging what is right and wrong) must be agreed. Every person and community is accountable to someone or something beyond themselves. (An atheist who, rightly, assumes that life should be valued and society be just is also tacitly nodding to this notion of accountability.) To be accountable must assume a discriminating set of values or standards – what we call morality or ethics. So although living ethically is not the sole preserve of religious people, Christians cannot escape the notion that our particular understanding of morality has to be rooted in our mortality as created beings.

From there, the narrative proposes that human beings are given a mandate to *cultivate*, which means to take culture (in its widest sense of growing, nurturing not only the material earth, but also the spirit – music, the arts and so on) seriously. It further means being responsible for the world of which we are co-creators with God, not exploiting and dominating, but stewarding and nurturing what we have as a given (and received) gift. Being 'made in the image of God' has many meanings, but it cannot mean less than taking co-responsibility for the material world.

'We seldom realize fully that we are sent to fulfill God-given tasks. We act as if we were simply dropped down in creation and have to decide to entertain ourselves until we die. But we were sent into the world by God, just as Jesus was. Once we start living our lives with that conviction, we will soon know what we were sent to do.'[6]
HENRI NOUWEN

'Anything created by human beings is already in the great book of nature.'[7]
ANTONI GAUDI

The Genesis poem (1–11) continues to explore the *destructiveness* of envy and rivalry, pointing to the nakedness of power hunger, and exposing both the glory of human beings in the created order and the misery of wrong moral choices by people of every age and stage. More could be said about Genesis, but space is short (unlike the 'space' of the universes, of course).

'. . . with every action, comment, conversation, we have the choice to invite Heaven or Hell to Earth.'[8]
ROB BELL

'The two things we all want so desperately — glory and relationship — can coexist only with God.'[9]
TIMOTHY KELLER

PSALMS AND PROPHETS

I have dared on many occasions to tell the story of the whole Bible in one minute. This can be done in different ways, but it arises from a concern that preachers and teachers assume everybody knows the 'big story', so they stick to expounding details. It's almost as if we could take a single frame from a stained-glass window and understand it without the wider context. Or read the third paragraph on page 121 of a novel and expect people to understand it. Without the bigger picture, it becomes possible to read into the Scriptures whatever pet dogma we prefer and then use it to exclude those who think differently.

Part of that story is the development over centuries of some understanding of what it means to be human – and to be God's people. And it all sounds so realistic when we set our own experiences against this unfolding account. For example, having been liberated (by God, not by their own power or ingenuity) from four centuries of slavery in Egypt, the people start to re-write their history very quickly. Wandering in the desert for forty years, they see a generation of nostalgia merchants die off. A new society could not be built by people who constantly looked back to a 'golden age'.

But before they enter their new land they are given instructions. They must build a society that enshrines justice, shows mercy to the poorest people, makes provision for those who are homeless and hungry, and takes mutual accountability seriously. Hence the establishment of annual rituals that will remind the people, through actions and not just words, that they were once slaves, for example. They must never treat other people as slaves, but this is precisely what they will do if they ever forget their own story. These rituals involve reciting a creed (such as in Deuteronomy 26) that accompanies sacrificial giving and asserts afresh that however hard they work at cultivating the earth, they do so in community.

'The Israelites' slavery in Egypt is the equivalent of our slavery to sin. God sent Moses to deliver them from bondage, and He sent Jesus Christ to set us free.'[10]
JOYCE MEYER

It is precisely the failure to play within these white lines that leads to the warnings of the prophets. They maintain, against popular contemporary assumptions, that forgetting who you are (created, mortal, accountable and so on) will eventually lead to the loss of all those things that you believe make you unique, special or chosen. Indeed, despite the warnings of the prophets, the people go into exile in the eighth and sixth centuries BC.

It is probably out of this experience of exile, disruption and alienation that Genesis 1–11 and many of the psalms give voice to grief and lament as well as praise and gratitude. As in creation, where order is brought out of chaos, how now might the 'order' of forgiveness, homecoming, 'newness after loss' (as Walter Brueggemann puts it) become real when all the evidence of our daily life tells us we have been conned, let down or abandoned by the very God who is supposed to be on our side?

'Lament is a cry of belief in a good God, a God who has His ear to our hearts, a God who transfigures the ugly into beauty. Complaint is the bitter howl of unbelief in any benevolent God in this moment, a distrust in the love-beat of the Father's heart.'[11]
ANN VOSKAMP

Vivid examples of this can be seen in Amos (warnings about a social order in which injustice is institutionalised), Isaiah (actually three books: warnings, hopes, shaping a new future back home), and psalms such as 137 (living with mockery in exile as 'reality' seems to rubbish faith). And as this narrative unfolds in the Old Testament, we begin to discern how a people struggled with how to live well, address challenges, deal with the downsides of human nature (we call it sin), and give voice to what we experience now when we feel hunted or marginalised. It is surely a tragedy that Jesus' hymnbook (the Psalms) is so rarely read in churches, where people cry out for a vocabulary of lament and hope as well as joy and praise.

'It is one thing to say with the prophet Amos, 'Let justice roll down like mighty waters,' and quite another to work out the irrigation system.'[12]
WILLIAM SLOANE COFFIN

'The Psalms wrap nouns and verbs around our pain better than any other book.'[13]
JONI EARECKSON TADA

THE NEW TESTAMENT

In the New Testament we find the story coming right down to earth. Literally. The words of creation in Genesis become the Word made flesh and living among us. What had always been the calling of the people who identified themselves as God's people was now to be fulfilled – enfleshed – in one man. But, as Jesus begins his public ministry, the people he draws around him embark on their own journey of recovering the narrative of God bringing order out of chaos. And this is a story of pain and bewilderment, not of gradual enlightenment. The disciples of Jesus often don't understand who he is, what he is doing, or what it all means. See Peter's reaction to Jesus stooping to wash his (soon to be) denier's feet at the last supper he shared with his friends.

'The first ministers were the twelve disciples. There is no evidence that Jesus chose them because they are brighter or nicer than other people. Their sole qualification seems to have been their initial willingness to rise to their feet when Jesus said, "Follow me."'[14]
FREDERICK BUECHNER

This, however, is where it begins to get properly encouraging for those of us who fear we fail at every point on the journey of living as a faithful human being, as described above. Jesus knows his friends and he is never surprised by their failures. He accepts their different personalities and priorities. He doesn't give them a theology exam before they can go walkabout with him. But neither does he let any of them veto the involvement of anyone else. Jesus does the calling; the disciples have to get on with it and with each other: that is their call and their witness.

So, underlying this story is the basic fact of community. No one follows Jesus, the Word made flesh, either alone or in the company only of people like them – or whom they like. Which is why the Church must never be a club of like-minded believers; it must always be made up of the awkward, the clever, the deniers, the doubters, the traitors, the bewildered, the joyful, the confused, the wounded and the healers. If the Church, at every level, comprises only people like me or people I like, then it is not a church.

'Jesus comes not for the super-spiritual but for the wobbly and the weak-kneed who know they don't have it all together, and who are not too proud to accept the handout of amazing grace.'[15]
BRENNAN MANNING

'All the persons of faith I know are sinners, doubters, uneven performers. We are secure not because we are sure of ourselves but because we trust that God is sure of us.'[16]
EUGENE H. PETERSON

Being human, then, means being human together. It means being accountable to God and each other. It means being a mess and not trying to resolve everyone else into reflecting my image rather than God's. And it means not being driven by fear (of immediate threat or confusion about the direction the world is going in), but being drawn by hope. Because Christian hope is, ultimately, rooted not in a formula for the survival of death, but rather in the person of God who raised Christ from the dead. That is what the biblical narrative exposes. And it is utterly realistic about what it looks and feels like to be mortal and moral in a contingent world while simultaneously being hopeful about redemption.

I note in conclusion that, in the vivid imagery of the book of Revelation, it is heaven that comes down to earth, not the other way around. God, we learn, has always taken the initiative: God creates and invites, seeks out Adam in the garden, calls a people to show who and how God is, takes choices and consequences seriously, never abandons the earth and its people, and opens our eyes to a bigger vision of what it can mean to live humanly as well as humanely on this earth.

'There is a part of you that is Love itself, and that is what we must fall into. It is already there. Once you move your identity to that level of deep inner contentment, you will realize you are drawing upon a Life that is much larger than your own and from a deeper abundance.'[17]
RICHARD ROHR

FOR DISCUSSION

1. Do you have experience – as an individual or as a church – of God bringing order out of chaos?

2. How might you square your own 'being human' with the demands of 'being human together'?

3. Can you give examples of where we adopt a pick'n'mix approach to the biblical narrative?

4. How might you tell the whole story of the Bible in one minute?

5. How might a conviction of common humanity influence your church's approach to priority setting, budgeting and outreach in the local community?

SESSION 3
BEING HUMAN

So what? That is not a bad question to ask of any survey of either the Bible or the world we live in. It is easy to identify problems and challenges – and, possibly, to apply one to the other. But theology has to be earthed if it is to be of any use. So in this session we need to bring the first two sessions together and see what it might look like if a Christian understanding of being human were to help shape a godly approach to some of the realities and challenges we face as a society.

We have seen that being human means being made in the image of God. When the poet of Psalm 8 sat under the stars and did some existentialist wondering, the vastness of the universe led not to a diminution of humanity, but to what might be called a confident humility. Rather than focus on the relative insignificance of any single mortal human being, the psalmist marvels that each person is noticed and supremely valued by the God who is 'sovereign'. And, it stands to reason, if every individual person matters eternally and infinitely, then every person matters equally.

'Don't undervalue yourself. God loves you. Your worth is what you are worth to God. Jesus died for you. You are of infinite value.'[1]
NICKY GUMBEL

This isn't some sort of raging anthropological exceptionalism that reduces the rest of creation to exploitable subservience. Rather, it is to heighten or emphasise not only the privilege of existence, but also the responsibility that goes with it.

'The life, beauty and meaning of the whole created order, from the tomtit to the Milky Way, refers back to the Absolute Life and Beauty of its Creator: and so lived, every bit has spiritual significance.'[2]
EVELYN UNDERHILL

'If unconditional love, loyalty, and obedience are the tickets to an eternal life, then my black Labrador, Venus, will surely be there long before me, along with all the dear animals in nature who care for their young at great cost to themselves and have suffered so much at the hands of humans.'[3]
RICHARD ROHR

But what it means to be made in the image of God is more complicated – or, better, more mysterious – than it appears at first glance. The God who breathes life into creation is ... er ... creative. His words are, 'Let there be ...' This God creates a world that, over the millennia, creates itself. Power is given away as humans share in the naming of the animals, the cultural mandate is issued, moral accountability for the care of the earth is guaranteed, and relationships of love create new generations of people made in God's likeness. Language – apparently unique to human beings – enables communication, self-reflection, and a need for classification. And these lead inexorably to the complexity of working out what 'Let there be' might mean for those charged with nurturing the earth.

Clearly, as we see with Adam and Eve, this also means working out the limits of what is 'let be' and when it is right, in accordance with the God whose image we bear, to say, 'Let there not be ...' Well, if this all seems a bit heavy, at least we should notice that God's way of creating was shot through with love, playfulness and joy. Otherwise, why would there be giraffes?

'The creation of something new is not accomplished by the intellect but by the play instinct acting from inner necessity. The creative mind plays with the objects it loves.'[4]
CARL JUNG

'There is no such thing as creative and non-creative people, only people who use their creativity and people who don't.'[5]
BRENÉ BROWN

However, as the narrative develops we begin to see what responsibility looks like. Despite the blame game that starts in the garden when Adam accuses Eve of causing the mess, the story focuses quickly on relationships. Adam and Eve are committed (condemned?) to living together and creating children. The children, Cain and Abel, are called to show what familial love can look like. Noah despairs of how the human experiment is turning out, but lives through the trauma of destruction. Then the tower of Babel shows how good (diversity) and bad (confusion and competition) life can be. And that concludes that part of the story.

Having expanded from the particular (Adam) to the 'global', the text then focuses down on one man and his story: Abram. And we get to follow these people through the beginning of their exploration of what it means to be a mortal human being seeking to look vaguely like the God in whose image we are made. And the story is not all good news.

Abram tries three times to pass his wife off as his sister in order to protect himself. His wife Sarai laughs at God and his crazy fantasies. However, when life continues to be fruitful, against all the odds, both people get a name change: Abram becomes Abraham and Sarai becomes Sarah. And this foreshadows what will become a striking feature of the scriptural narrative: God does not leave us trapped in what we are or have been – our failures or reputations, for example – but gives us the name that, literally, personifies who we might become.

Key to this is the invention of covenant. Instead of simply dictating to people what they should be – a bit like robots that can be programmed to behave in a particular way – God takes people and their freedom (to choose) seriously. His faithfulness to humanity, born of self-giving love, is guaranteed, but the deal is that people must behave towards God and each other as God has behaved towards them.

'The people who related to God best – Abraham, Moses, David, Isaiah, Jeremiah – treated him with startling familiarity. They talked to God as if he were sitting in a chair

beside them, as one might talk to a counselor, a boss, a parent, or a lover. They treated him like a person.'[6]
PHILIP YANCEY

Now, it doesn't take either reason or imagination to see where this is going. Isn't it remarkable that all the great heroes of the faith turn out to be moral disasters? The apostle Paul might single out Abraham as the father of the faith, but try being Abraham's wife in the episodes mentioned earlier. Moses eventually becomes the vehicle of liberation, but he has also been a murderer and a coward. Whomever we meet in Scripture, they all turn out to be the sort of people most of us wouldn't choose to lead a church. If you don't believe me, work your way through the disciples of Jesus.

'David, Moses, Saul of Tarsus, these were all people who did terrible terrible things ... The Bible would be a lot shorter without grace.'[7]
SHANE CLAIBORNE

So, from the beginning of our narrative, human beings – created in God's image and sought out by a God who always takes the initiative towards people – look remarkably like you and me. Their individual and collective failures are all too predictable and all too human. And still God doesn't give up and walk away. That's the story of what it means to be human.

This is why I used the phrase 'confident humility' earlier. Being human in a complex world of relationships and competing cultures demands of those made in God's image that they see human beings as God sees them – infinitely loved and valued – while recognising the disasters we all create all the time. Confident in God and God's humanity, humble in being realistic about our need for redemption and restoration – to see this played out over centuries we need to read the prophets of the Old Testament. Promise is always accompanied by accountability: if you behave in a way that does not reflect the image of God, then don't be surprised if you lose the things that make you who you are. (A bit like not being surprised if the fruit stops growing when you have cut the trunk from its roots.)

'Humility is the most difficult of all virtues to achieve;
nothing dies harder than the desire to think well of self.'[8]
T. S. ELIOT

'Christianity does not think of man finally submitting to the
power of God, it thinks of him as finally surrendering to
the love of God. It is not that man's will is crushed, but that
man's heart is broken.'[9]
WILLIAM BARCLAY

Now, this brings us to a place where we briefly need to put a bit
of flesh on the ideas we have been exploring. What might it look
like for Christians in the UK in the second quarter of the twenty-
first century to reflect the image of God and live the life of eternity
(in terms of quality not quantity, of course) in our world now? A
quick preamble, then we can look at one or two examples.

In 2021 the Roman Catholic Bishops' Conference of England
and Wales contributed a paper to the Conference on the Future
of Europe. Before identifying particular issues for discussion, the
paper quoted Pope Francis's call in October 2017 to 'put the
human person at the centre of all we do'. Not economics, politics
or ideologies, but people. Putting humans at the centre necessarily
means shaping politics, economics and ideologies that are
humane. But where the ideology or search for power diminishes
human beings, then something has gone wrong somewhere. As I
have often remarked in the House of Lords, economics are there to
serve people – the common good; people are not there to serve
economics, a cog in someone else's ideological wheel.

'The challenge today is to convince people of the value of
truth, honesty, compassion and a concern for others.'[10]
DALAI LAMA

So, what do we do about refugees or asylum seekers, for
example, if we take this seriously? What is the balance to be
struck between, for example, the sanctity of human life on the
one hand and border security on the other? Yes, making choices
means negotiating between principle and policy. But in the same

way as a budget can be thought of as theology by numbers, so might our response to poor people be considered theology by identity. I'll try to explain briefly.

One of the curses over the last century has been the tendency of certain societies to categorise people. Only by categorising them can they be dehumanised to the point where they can be got rid of. The Nazis dehumanised the Jews, Gypsies, communists and homosexuals. They could then be processed efficiently through gas chambers as if they were things. The genocide in Rwanda was generated by people regarding the tribal 'other' as cockroaches – and what do we do with cockroaches? We have seen it with Islamic State and other entities that seek power at all costs. The conflicts in Ukraine, Gaza and Sudan bear the same fingerprints. Much of the mass migration we see across the globe is driven by these same dynamics – and the people we see on the move are those who have been told they are not human, do not count and are expendable.

Is this how I would want my own children to be considered? Or myself? Or, perish the thought, my enemies whom Jesus asks me to love?

'The way of acquiescence leads to moral and spiritual suicide. The way of violence leads to bitterness in the survivors and brutality in the destroyers. But, the way of nonviolence leads to redemption and the creation of the beloved community.'[11]
MARTIN LUTHER KING, JR

So, being human is not easy. Being accountable to God and each other is even harder. And that is the tension in which Christians, among all other human beings, are caught up.

When we created the brand new Anglican Diocese of Leeds in 2014 we eventually landed on three values: loving, living and learning. These three words contain our theology within a confident humility. We *love* God, the world of God's creation and our neighbour as ourselves. We *live* in the world, as it is, but are drawn by a vision of how it might be – what we call the kingdom of God. We are incarnational, committed to the now. And we are humble enough to know that we will get it wrong time and time again, but we will *learn* and try to grow, never pretending to be right at all costs, but honest enough to hold our hands up in exposed guilt. It seems to me that these values aren't bad ones for any Christian body.

'God's aim in human history is the creation of an inclusive community of loving persons, with himself included as its primary sustainer and most glorious inhabitant.'[12]
DALLAS WILLARD

Christians, then, must be people who reflect in word and action the nature of the God who has made us all in his image. In one sense, the equation is simple: if we are to be truly human and truly Christian, we must look something like the Jesus we read about in the gospels. If we genuinely accept Paul's image that we are the 'body of Christ', there is no other criterion by which we can be judged. And to treat other people or peoples in any way that does not reflect the God and Father of Jesus himself means that we are a living fraud. To put it bluntly, our political, economic and social priorities must be shaped essentially by our theology and not the other way round.

'If you want to know who God is, look at Jesus. If you want to know what it means to be human, look at Jesus. If you want to know what love is, look at Jesus. If you want to know what grief is, look at Jesus. And go on looking until you're not just a spectator, but you're actually part of the drama which has him as the central character.'[13]
N. T. WRIGHT

This means being caught up in the tension between what we might call 'the wind of the Spirit' and the winds of the world – and not constantly trying to run away from the discomfort. Which is why the Church can be an uncomfortable place to inhabit. It's also why in our final session we shall look at what this tells us about Advent, Christmas and the rest of the story.

FOR DISCUSSION

1. Are your/our priorities fired by our understanding of God's nature and call, or the other way round?

2. How might you answer someone who says that being Christian in this way is naive or impractical?

3. What does the Jesus of the gospels look like? And what might the Church look like if it looked like him?

4. Do you see yourself as made in the image of God? If so, what do you think this means?

5. Can you think of examples where seeing people as made in God's image makes you very uncomfortable or conflicted?

SESSION 4
PLAYING A PART (NOT PLAYING APART)

There is an underlying logic to a biblical understanding of what it means to be human and what it is to be a follower of Jesus. The basic fact of our humanity is that we are made in the image of God. As people who know we don't live up to that privilege very well, we are called to follow Jesus as his friends and disciples, walking with him through the chances and changes of ordinary life and discovering – if our eyes and ears are open and our curiosity is tickled – what God, the world and we look like when seen through his eyes. But our discipleship must be derived from and build up our humanity. If our discipleship diminishes our humanity or that of others, it is not discipleship of the Jesus we read about in the gospels.

'Discipleship is the process of becoming who Jesus would be if he were you.'[1]
DALLAS WILLARD

'The Bible itself does not seem too bothered by the idea that talking of God suffering might in any way diminish God, or detract from his perfection. On the contrary, the Bible seems to revel in the richness of describing God in ways that reflect our own human realities.'[2]
CHRISTOPHER J. H. WRIGHT

I could add here that any ministry I exercise belongs to God, is mediated through the Church and exercised by me. But the vocation is God's, not mine. It can be taken away. It is not a possession to be held or a commodity to be traded. This ministry must be derived from my discipleship, which is rooted in my humanity. If that dynamic gets messed up, and my discipleship is contained only in my exercise of ministry, for example, then something has gone seriously wrong. It will lead to trouble, just as in the Old Testament the people went into exile because they had taken God for granted and lost their basic vocation: to lay down their own lives in order that the world might know who and how God is.

So, what we are dealing with here is serious business. The Christian seeks to be more like Jesus, and Jesus shows us what it is to be (like) God. It is, then, about God, not us. Yet in a world that is going through a human identity crisis, we can see quite easily how the Church can begin to reflect the current assumption that it is really all about 'me'. We are looking in the wrong direction.

agree

If you don't believe me, try looking at the words of many contemporary worship songs. The focus seems to be on God making me feel better about myself. The power of worshipping God for who God is and what God is about too easily gets lost as an end in itself. And this observation throws up some difficult questions.

'The message of some churches today seems to be, "Only sing if it appeals to your sense of style, or your demographic." Yet when we look at heaven, we see that every tribe and every nation will sing together.'[3]
KEITH GETTY

When Paul appeals to the Christians in Rome (12:1–2) with: 'by the mercies of God ... present your bodies as a living sacrifice, holy and acceptable to God' he calls this their 'spiritual worship'. So, no spirituality that is not embodied. Spiritual worship that ignores the real, concrete, social and material context of the worshippers is neither worship nor spiritual. But Paul goes on to thicken the plot: 'Do not be conformed to this world, but be transformed by the renewing of your minds, so that you may discern what is the will of God'.

Rom 12:1–

So body, mind and spirit can't be separated into compartments and treated in isolation from one another. No fragmentation or convenient distraction here. As James recognises in his letter, the reality or integrity of your spirituality will be judged according to your handling of the material world, including your body, which will in turn be shaped by how your mind is being changed so that, increasingly, you see through God's eyes.

'The spiritual life of individuals has to be extended both vertically to God and horizontally to other souls; and the more it grows in both directions, the less merely individual and therefore more truly personal it will become.'[4]
EVELYN UNDERHILL

Why have I laboured this point here? Well, simply because what we have learned in the first three sessions of this course is that being truly human means being embodied, learning to look and see and think differently, and being together on the journey. To be blunt: Jesus does the calling in the gospels and doesn't give any of the other 'called' a veto over who else comes along. We are in it together. The witness of the Church in a fragmenting world is not to do with maintaining our purity from those who look and see and think differently, but rather to demonstrate to this world what it looks like to follow Jesus together – because we are all made in the image of God and are all called to reflect the Jesus we say we follow. If Jesus shows us what it looks like to be truly human, then we have no option but to stick with him and his ragbag of friends.

'This is what God's kingdom is like: a bunch of outcasts and oddballs gathered at a table, not because they are rich or worthy or good, but because they are hungry, because they said yes. And there's always room for more.'[5]
RACHEL HELD EVANS

This takes us back to an observation made in the last session: the three words beginning with 'L' – 'loving', 'living' and 'learning' – that very simply encapsulate who we in the Diocese of Leeds think we are, and what and whom we are here for. Basically, we *love* God, the worlds of his creation and our neighbour as ourselves. We *live* in the world as it is, but are being drawn by a vision of how it might be (the kingdom of God). And we know we'll mess it up a million times, so we take the risks and *learn* as we go, with no embarrassment when we fail or get it wrong.

But these values simply shape a dynamic that we've owned from day one: as I put it at the time, we want to be a *vibrant* diocese,

vibrating between the wind of the Spirit and the winds of the real
world in which God has put us for this time. But this means being
willing to be caught up in that tension and not constantly using our
energy to try to escape from it. This is the reality Jesus calls us into.
It will not be resolved this side of eternity, so we'd better get used
to it.

> 'Having a Christian worldview means being utterly
> convinced that biblical principles are not only true but also
> work better in the grit and grime of the real world.'[6]
> NANCY PEARCEY

Of course, this emphasises the point referred to in the first session
of this course that some of the more recent phenomena that
question our understandings of or assumptions about what it
means to be human demand new consideration. In a Church
where the emphasis is too often on 'me' ('My Jesus, my Saviour'),
how do we recover the fact that (a) we are all embodied and (b)
it is more about 'us' than 'me'? Human beings are social animals.
We need one another. And the genius of the gospel, as Jesus
commanded, is that we stick together in a fragmented world. No
wonder he prayed for the unity of his friends before his enemies
killed him, and his friends abandoned him.

Being human, then, must mean taking responsibility, along with
others whom we haven't chosen, for the witness and life of
the Church – at every level. In the words Jesus' friends said to
Bartimaeus when leaving Jericho: 'Take heart; get up, he is calling
you' (Mark 10:49).

> 'Holiness grows so fast where there is kindness. The world
> is lost for want of sweetness and kindness. Do not forget we
> need each other.'[7]
> MOTHER TERESA

This brings us towards some conclusions that find their theological
roots in this time of year, Advent. Advent is a time when we look
forward, anticipating a future that will surprise us and upset
our prejudices. Living through Advent means setting aside our
certainties and laying ourselves open to new possibilities. After all,

the irruption of God incarnate into the real world didn't occur as anybody might have preconceived it.

> 'Something ultimate has entered our world, something or Someone that calls us to attention, calls us out of our daily preoccupations and our routine points of view. That is what this season with its special biblical readings is designed to reveal.'[8]
> FLEMING RUTLEDGE

[handwritten margin note: Badly phrased. Should be God's Love but...]

The biblical story is one of God's people failing to take heart, get up and hear God's authentic call; to embody in person and society who God is and what God is about. The call to lay down one's life became a matter of assumed privilege. The call to be responsibly creative – have dominion in – gradually turned into domination of creation. The call to justice and ethical generosity slid into corruption and self-justifying partiality. The call to 'sing the LORD's song in a foreign land' (Psalm 137:4) became a resentful demand that one version of the Lord's song be the only one heard.

So, what was the expectation of the people of Jesus' society? The gospels, in various ways, make it clear that popular expectations of the coming of God might involve something more impressive than a baby being born in obscurity, a child being made a refugee in a land resonant with historical curse, a man being pursued and eventually nailed to a gallows on a trumped-up charge. But these expectations were confounded in the gospel story. God wants us to conform to his image, not force him to conform to ours.

In this sense, God will come among us as one of us, but on his terms alone. Incarnate in the real world of time and space, God subjects himself to the uncertainties, joys, cruelties and injustices of the world we know too well. Jesus lays down his life, thus fulfilling what had always been the calling of God's people, and inviting his people to follow him down this same road. 'Come and get crucified' would not win as a populist slogan of a political party, but it is the mantra of this God whom we meet in Jesus of Nazareth.

'Our Lord wanted us to be Christ-like. Christ-like doesn't mean not having faults. It means that you do actually have a capacity to draw out the good that is in others.'[9]
DESMOND TUTU

BEING HUMAN CHRISTIANLY?

The story that began in the explosion of light of the world's first day has continued – God's people being called to show the world who and how God is by embodying the unique vocation that has never changed. Thus it is that being truly human is to reflect what we see in Jesus himself. The gospels show us that he is free from the constraints of expectations of success, privilege or personal gain; he lives in the company of others who fail repeatedly in their vocation to be his disciples and friends; he sees the present in the context of eternity; he loves what doesn't always merit love, is gracious where mercy looks feeble, and he looks for the greatness of the small in seeds of love and grace and mercy sown in a complicated world overrun by weeds.

Like a stone on the surface of a still river
Driving the ripples on forever
Redemption rips through the surface of time
In the cry of a tiny babe[10]
BRUCE COCKBURN

'Jesus' coming is the final and unanswerable proof that God cares.'[11]
WILLIAM BARCLAY

In our first session we took a brief look at some of the challenges human beings face today on a fragile planet in a conflicted world. Technology trails morality in its ever-longer wake. Climate change confronts us with crisis – literally the judgement that demands a responsible and accountable choosing. Migration shows us the face of people made in the image of God and compels us to ask what we might expect from Christians if we were the migrant. Conflict draws us into the hard ethics of defence and attack, and what price is paid by whom for our security. Technology raises for us questions of who is in charge, who sets the priorities, who is ultimately responsible for how the world is. And AI confronts us with the question of what it means for human beings to be embodied – with all the implications for conversation, relationship, power and character.

In conclusion, I mentioned earlier that I visited Sudan in mid-2024 with a colleague. Why did I go against government advice and fly into a war zone when we have Zoom, FaceTime, phones and emails? The answer is simply that sometimes these options are not enough. Being human means being present – physically touching, facing. Embracing our brothers and sisters in a displacement camp cannot be done remotely. Being human means accepting the limitations and the richly unique joys of being there.

Being human ultimately means being like Jesus ... being Jesus for those among whom we live and to whom we belong.

'Be who God meant you to be and you will set the world on fire.'[12]
ST CATHERINE OF SIENA

FOR DISCUSSION

1. What sort of Jesus are you waiting for during Advent?

2. As Jesus enters the world at Christmas, how prepared are you for the journey with him, listening and learning, watching and engaging as you go?

3. What single thing might you do this Christmas for people made in God's image whose experience is one of having that image ignored?

4. Which of the issues we have looked at in this course do you think you might take more seriously – and practically – as you follow Jesus into the new year?

5. What might your church look like if it looked like Jesus?

TRANSCRIPT
INTRODUCTION

NICK B	Hello, and welcome to this York Course for Advent. The theme is *Who am I?* What does it mean to be a human being in the real world in which we live? A very profound question; one that we'll be knocking around in various ways, over four sessions.
	Now, I'm Nick Baines. I'm the Bishop of Leeds in the Church of England, and I'm joined by a couple of friends who are going to join in the conversation. So perhaps you'd like to introduce yourselves.
NICK S	Hi, I'm Nick Spencer. I work as Senior Fellow at the Christian think tank, Theos. I'm an Essex boy by birth, but I live in Surrey now. (I've moved up in the world, clearly.) I'm married to Kate and have two adult kids, Ellen and Johnny.
CHINE	And my name's Chine McDonald. I am Director of the religion and society think tank, Theos. I'm also a writer and broadcaster. And I live in southeast London with my husband Mark, and my two young boys.
NICK B	So, we have a variety of identities and perspectives. I should have added that I'm from Liverpool originally and to Liverpool I shall return. And I'm a father and a grandfather as well.
	So, we'll be looking through these different lenses as we go forward. So, we look forward to seeing you in session 1

SESSION 1
WHO AM I?

NICK B	Welcome to the first session of this Advent York Course. It's asking a great question; *Who am I?* It's a question that underlies everyone's thinking about what it is to be a human being. Who am I? Why do I matter? So, we're going to be talking about that. And I wonder if I could first of all go to you, Nick. Who are you?
NICK S	There's so many different ways of answering that question, Nick. But my go-to place would be to define myself according to the relationships I have with different people. So, I'm Kate's husband. I'm Johnny and Ellen's dad.
NICK B	Right. And you could add much more to that as well. How about you, Chine?
CHINE	Yes. Similarly, I am a mother and a wife. I'm also a Londoner, but also, uh, come from somewhere else, which is Nigeria. And in Nigeria, when you ask who you are, you talk about where you come from; who your people are. So, I'm Igbo, I'm from the southeast of Nigeria. But I'm also a Londoner.
NICK B	So, I mean, what we've uncovered already is that we have multiple identities and we, in one sense, we layer them.
	So, the question, who am I?, is not as simple as it sounds right at the outset. Let's move it on to . . . What is it that gets you up in the morning? What are you living for? Or do you just exist?
CHINE	I'm in a really lucky position to do a job that feels to me like it is also my calling. I have a sense of vocation, which is to communicate the good news of the Christian faith to a world that doesn't understand it.
	So, every day I get to do that through my job as being Director of Theos, which is a religion and society think tank. And yeah, I'm lucky in that both of those things align. My kind of sense of purpose and mission also aligns with the thing that I get paid for – to get up for every morning.

But, before I go to work, I am a mother; have got to get things ready. I'm living for . . . often it feels like the school timetable. And what I need to pack in my children's bags or what I need to do for nursery. So, I'm living for the people around me and my family, but also the sense of calling that I have.

NICK B   Do you ever get lost . . . while meeting the needs of everyone else? 'Cause a lot of mothers do say this. You know, you get a few years in and then you think, well, who am I?

CHINE   That is, that is a really . . . Yes, I do, because I think a lot of what I do is for them, and it's for my husband. And those are the first things that I think about when I wake up. It is how am I going to serve them, in effect, how am I going to make sure that they're okay? But also, my kind of sense of wider family. Because it's not just my immediate family that are the thing that I'm embedded in, but my kind of wider global network of family. So, you know, it's my cousin's wedding in Nigeria soon. I've been sent a list about the things I need to buy for her. Um, I need to check in on my grandmother, check in on my parents.

And then there's also my team of people that I work with every day, as well as my kind of friends, who are also going through some really difficult things at the moment. So, there are lots of kind of people that I'm concerned about, and there isn't enough time in the day to also sometimes think about myself. But that's kind of, that's, that's fine for me.

NICK B   It's complex, isn't it? And actually, dealing with difficult things is the norm, not the aberration in human life. What about you, Nick? What do you live for?

NICK S   The strange thing is that I'm at the kind of slightly the other end of the family spectrum, Chine. So, my wife and I are empty nesters. I mean, temporarily (the kids come back; they're at university). But, actually, the same problem of questioning who you are affects you at *that* end of the family life.

Because I was a stay-at-home dad for some of the time when the kids were very little, and we invested a lot of time with the kids. And you do all the things you do with kids, and you know who you are, then. You're dad and you, you know, I was, I was touchline dad. I mean, I spent many, many hours on the touchline. I didn't like sport, but when your son's playing, you're fully invested!

Brilliant. Really, really good. And they go and it's great. You want them to go off, you want them to form their own life and so on and so forth. And then you wake up in the morning and they're not there, and you think, 'Hmm, so who am I exactly today?' Which is another way of asking, 'Who am I there to live for?' Now, of course, there are lots and lots of answers to that, but the one that's been dominant in your life for many, many years is no longer quite so dominant. And that requires a bit of a cognitive shift.

NICK B   I'd have answered it quite differently actually, the question. Because, if I can make a statement, I think the beginning of freedom as a human being, of knowing who you are, is to recognise your mortality. That I am someone who will die.

The day after we record this, I'm having heart surgery. I've already had brain surgery, you know, and you come to terms with the fact that you're a mortal human being. And that's the beginning of freedom. And particularly for Christians who start further down the line, as if God is there to make my life comfortable, then that can be a problem.

But in fact, who am I? I'm a mortal human being made in the image of God, and the rest is detail. You know, when you're about to go under the anaesthetic, that's what you hold onto, it seems to me.

But the, the world we're living in is quite complicated. It's threatening. The twenty-first century is not continuing with the optimism with which it began.

And we see conflict in a lot of places as well. We've got the threat of climate change. And in the midst of all of that, there is this question, what does it mean to be a human? And I wonder how, in that context, how would you begin to answer that or address it?

NICK S   Well, given where we started, that there are lots of different ways of answering that question. I think you would begin to think about where you are when you're answering it. So, you talked about your mortality then. We are recording this a few days after the election of Pope Leo XIV. He interestingly remarked, a few days after his election, that he chose the name Leo the XIV in homage to Leo the XIII, who was Pope at the end of the nineteenth century at the period of really significant industrial upheaval. He chose Leo XIV because he said he's living in a similar time of industrial upheaval, where AI threatens to change, improve, challenge so much of what we do. And this presents itself as a challenge not only to what we do, but who we are. 'Cause if you have AI that is able to process information *vastly* faster than we are able to, and if we're moving towards what's known as AGI, artificial general intelligence, which is machines being able to do stuff, physical stuff that they kind of determine as opposed to stuff that we give them to do, it forces on us the question, well, how are they different from us? And what makes us special? And having written a bit about this, I think the answer to that comes a lot down to what you were talking about now – our mortality or our fallibility or vulnerability; our embodiedness and our embeddedness, and all these qualities. The fact that we are creatures that, as it were, *grasp* for eternity, but are nonetheless very much bounded by mortality. I think that is a critical thing to get into our heads at a time, in an age, in which the question of who are we – in the light of technology – is going to keep on coming up.

NICK B   We'll come back to that in a moment. But Chine, I mean, how do you respond to that? . . . The . . . especially the rise of AI, of technology, where in the past there's always been human agency. At the end of the day, there's human agency. And the fear now – it seems quite widespread – that that becomes removed when you have machines that can think for themselves. So, what's the difference?

CHINE   Yeah, I think about the two things being linked in terms of kind of mortality and AI and the kind of technological advancements. And I think about the billionaires who are on these quests for eternal life or immortality. So, these very, very rich men, often, who get up at 4.00 a.m., who eat three mouthfuls of food a day, who are constantly being tested to make sure that their bodies are at their kind of optimum level so that they can live forever, apparently.

And I think that there is something about the body, the human body, as distinct from an AI or a robot or a 'thing', that makes me realise that what's different from *me*, and the kind of technology as it stands now, is that actually bodies are also important. We are not just minds. We're not just things, um, that can think quickly, can, kind of do maths, uh, very quickly. We are also bodies, and our bodies are located in places and in families and in times and cultures. So, I think the body is also an important part of who we are as human beings.

NICK B   Which is at the heart of Christian faith because at Christmas, God opts into the world, the material world, and Christianity is a material faith. It does wind me up sometimes when people talk about spirituality, as if it was a separated thing, when we have to be earthed – that's what incarnation is all about.

CHINE   I think for me, the closest I have felt to my own mortality is in the labour ward, giving birth – twice. It is the time in which I have felt most like a body. And the early years of parenting for me have been very embodied experiences too – complete and utter devotion, touch, love, care for another human being's body. And I think what I've learned through that – that very bodily experience – is also something very spiritual, which is about love. What love is. The love of God towards us, and how we can show love towards other human beings as well.

NICK S   Just to kind of chip in there as well.

NICK B   Yeah, sure.

NICK S   One other critical aspects of being human is being

creative. The image of God, we've already mentioned, and Genesis 1, which is a phrase that has been analysed to death by theology over the years. One of the familiar interpretations for it is that we are made in the image of a creative God, because you get this phrase after God is doing a lot of creating.

That invites the question, what is creativity? Now you are probably familiar with Nick Cave, the famous singer/songwriter who's been in this space a lot. And very interestingly, recently, he has his website called *The Red Hand Diaries*, and he answers responses to fans there.

A fan in New Zealand sent him the lyrics of a song that he'd asked ChatGPT to write in the style of Nick Cave. And Nick Cave responded in quite a robust way, that I probably won't repeat on, on, in our discussion here. But he basically said it was complete nonsense. Why was it nonsense? Because it was a burlesque. Creativity, he says, is an attempt to achieve transcendence. But ChatGPT can't *transcend* anything because it hasn't *been* anywhere. It hasn't *done* anything. It hasn't *suffered any limits*. And Nick Cave, who has famously lost two sons, you know, borne unbelievable grief, talking about the grief and the finitude and the vulnerability and the contingency of human life – is critical to what it is but also our simultaneous desire to grasp the beyond, of being aware of what we would clumsily call eternity – that is a deeply creative aspect of our character. But you have to be embodied and embedded and contingent and fragile in order to achieve it in the first place. So, you get this brilliant tension between our vulnerability and our fragility and our transcendence as humans.

NICK B It takes me back to that other question that's framed slightly differently in Genesis chapter 3, where Adam and Eve do the naughty stuff. And then their instinct is not to go and find God, find the transcendent, find the eternal – their instinct is to hide. And it's God who takes the initiative and comes walking in the garden in the cool of the day, it says, and then asks this question,

'Adam, where *are* you?' Immortal human being, *where are* you? And the, 'Where are you?,' it seems to me, is a very good accompaniment to the 'Who are you?' You don't know who you are until you know where you are. And where you are is embodied.

So, there's a lot here, when we ask a simple question, who am I? We can use our identifiers. I'm from Liverpool. I'm a husband. I'm a grandfather. All of that sort of stuff we talked about, but we go deeper and deeper. And we find out that we are embodied children of God.

Thank you very much.

We hope you've enjoyed that first session, that first conversation. We look forward to seeing you in session two, and the theme then is, what does the Bible say about this sort of stuff?

SESSION 2
WHAT DOES THE BIBLE SAY?

NICK B   Welcome to session two of the 2025 Advent York Course, with this theme, rooted in a question, *Who am I?* What does it mean to be a human being? And this session, we're going to be asking, well, 'What does the Bible say?' I mean, every human being works with a narrative, whether they articulate it or not, that roots their understanding of who they are and why they matter.

I remember at university, where we were studying existentialism. One of my friends was a very ardent existentialist, and one day I put my fingers against his head and said, 'I've got a gun. I'm going to shoot your head off. Tell me why I shouldn't.'

He said, 'I don't want you to.'

I said, 'Well, no, it doesn't matter. I'm going to authenticate my existence by *choosing* to do this.' And I said, 'Give me another one.'

He said, 'It'll make a mess on the carpet.'

I said, 'That actually is a better answer!' [Laughter.]

You know, why do we think we matter? There's something underneath, that, against which we measure our meaning. So, I mean, Christians would say that the, the meaning of human life is rooted in God, who is love and who is creative – stuff we began to explore in the first session.

I wonder if you could just say a bit about what you understand love to be.

CHINE   Now, this is a big question, this one!

When I think about love, I think about . . . almost an unconditional positive regard – um, my husband's a social worker, so he talks about this a lot – this regard for another human being that goes beyond whether they are annoying on a particular day, um, whether you agree with their politics, whether they are kind of misbehaving in some way. It is a sense of positivity towards them, a sense of, uh, love, compassion, care that can't actually be measured. And it's intangible, but it expresses itself through acts of love. Loving acts, including listening, taking care of and not wanting to overpower. And love is complicated, but it's . . . I think how we see another person gets us towards what we might understand love to be.

NICK B   But some people will talk about God as love in a rather sentimental way, as if love was something airy fairy or just to do with feelings, that sort of thing. I wonder, Nick, in the biblical narrative, what does this tell us about who we are in relation to a God who says God is love?

NICK S   The love that you experience through the stories and the Scriptures isn't sentimental. It's quite the opposite. In fact, this is a possibly slightly grim thing to mention, but it, it looks a bit like what your friend threatened when you put a gun to his head. It's very messy. And what we get in the New Testament is actually bloody as well. So intuitively that doesn't make sense. How can something that is supposed to make you so warm and fuzzy and kind and comfortable be so superficially, so challenging and so ugly?

And it's because love is gift, in my mind, essentially. It's the gift of the self to the other; it's recognising where the good of the other lies and being prepared to pursue it, including giving what I have and *who I am* to that good. And pursued to its *extreme*, that means giving myself for the other, even when that means sacrificing my life, as Christ does, in the most total, and in that instance, painful way. Now it's an extreme example of what love is, and just because, you know, you haven't been crucified for people in your life, doesn't mean you don't love them.

But it's, as it were, the light that leads us on to what our true fulfilment as human persons is, which is to give ourselves for the good of the other.

NICK B   I was doing a wedding the other day, and I don't do many these days. In fact, the last one I did, I think, was for my daughter, which was a long time ago. And I was saying to the congregation there that you see people come in at a wedding with cards and wrapping paper with silver and pink, little fluffy love hearts and it's, you know, lovely.

And I said, I'm not sure that's an icon of love. *This* is an icon of love. It's a man nailed to a cross. Arms open, embracing the world and saying, throw at me what you will, and I won't throw it back. That's a sort of hard-edged – takes us back to the first session – which is that spirituality, love, whatever you want to talk about, has to be earthed in the material.

NICK S I mean, we are famously limited in English, which is in some ways such an extraordinarily rich language, by only really having one word that we use for love. New Testament Greek famously has four to describe very different kind of relationships. We have love, so, we then use the same word to describe, you know, cuddles at bedtime, sexual love and sacrificial love. You're asking it to do a lot of work then really.

NICK B Yeah!

CHINE I think there is also something about the idea of God's love in the Christian story that gets to this idea that Nick talked about, which is gift, and that gift being freely given without expectation of return.

Now I think in a lot of the human relationships that we have, when we talk about love, sometimes the love is tied to how someone looks, whether they are kind to you back, um, whether you agree with them. But actually, love is gift in that it is without all of those kind of other restrictions or receiving back. In the kind of social-work sector, in some professions, there is talk of professional love, and that helps me understand this idea that love is actually a decision and sometimes it's a responsibility to keep loving, keep acting in a loving way, keep choosing to love despite how we feel, despite the kind of fluffy stuff that we see so vividly, imagine in the kind of early marriage or romantic love. It is a decision to keep showing up.

NICK B In the last eight months I've been in both Sudan and Iraq, where the stories of people there, for example, in Iraq, uh, visiting the Yazidis, listening to the stories of horror . . . How is it credible to talk about a God of love in a world in which people, who presumably God loves, suffer the most appalling injustices?

CHINE   Well, this is the great question of the human experience. It is, how can we explain this love, despite all the terrible things that are going on? Now, it might sound glib, but I think it is human beings acting in unloving ways that cause a lot of these wars and conflict; a decision by humans to have power, to have control, to have what other people have, and to not see each other as loved people made in the image of a God.

Now, I think for those people who are in those really profound places of suffering, the hope that I find, as someone observing that, is often the stories of profound love and care, even despite the circumstances that people are in. There is still loving acts. There are still acts of courage and selflessness that demonstrate the beauty of God's love, I think.

But it's, it's a really difficult one to try and explain, especially for those who have lost their lives or who've lost the lives of their loved ones.

NICK S   Just to pick up on what Chine said there, and actually picking up on the wording of your question, which I think I'm right in saying was, 'How is it possible to talk about God in those situations?'

I think the answer is it isn't. It isn't possible to *talk* about God in those situations. It might be possible to *act* like God in those situations, and in fact, *talking* about God in those situations, without any commensurate act, is horrible. Frankly, the person that goes into a war zone, or a children's cancer hospital, or anything like that, and tries to *justify* – by logic – what is happening there should be shown the door very quickly.

In those situations, you don't *talk* about what's happening. You *do* something.

NICK B   Which again, is deeply Christian because at the heart of Christian faith is God who is embodied into where all the mess is the most acute. Not just with words, but, you know, embodied presence, and then suffers the injustices and the, you know, the vagaries and the horrors of all of that can mean.

NICK S   And I thought about that this Easter, and I've no doubt this is a more of a reflection on me than on Christian theology, but I thought about, I prefer Good Friday to Easter Sunday! Which is a strange thing to say, 'cause of course, Easter Sunday superficially, is a much more joyful day. There's much more to celebrate there.

But there are times when you might find yourself at an Easter Sunday service thinking, 'Really?'

NICK B   Yeah.

NICK S   Whereas I never found myself in a Good Friday service thinking, 'Really?' Because a Good Friday service *resonates* with me, particularly maybe because of the way the world is at the moment. I'm obviously not suggesting that you can't have the two together, because if you don't have Easter Sunday without Good Friday, the torturers win. That's the bottom line. But just in terms of *resonating* how we feel – and certainly how I feel about the world sometimes – Good Friday does, powerfully.

NICK B   And Easter Day doesn't fix Good Friday, which is, you know, the tendency.

Let's . . . It used to drive me mad as a kid in a church in Liverpool, that Good Friday . . . there was no silence or anything, you know. You, you sang about the cross, but it was the victory of the cross. And then Saturday, you'd just sort of go shopping or endure it. [Laughter.]

And then Sunday, 'Oh, thank goodness, you know, we've got it.' Or even on Friday you'd be singing the songs of triumph. It always seems to me, and I said this in the cathedral recently, on Easter morning, you know, the priest comes out and says, 'Hallelujah, Christ is risen.' And the congregation replies, 'He is risen indeed. Hallelujah.' And I think we shouldn't. I think the priest should say, 'Hallelujah. Christ is risen.' And the congregation should say, '*What?*' [Everyone laughs.] Because what we read in the gospel is bewilderment.

NICK S   Yeah.

NICK B   Fear. And they begin a process then of trying to work out . . . like the two on the road to Emmaus . . . our theology, our understanding of Scripture and all of that, doesn't work out when Messiah dies. And Jesus, the risen Jesus says, 'Can I put this story back together in a different way?'

NICK S   Hmm.

NICK B   Which is why their hearts burn within them as they walk to Emmaus.

NICK S   Mmm. Yeah. I mean, the resurrection appearances are bewildering. They're not ordered.

NICK B   No.

NICK S   They're not kind of schematised and planned. And there's a lot of 'work it out yourself here'.

NICK B   Yeah.

NICK S   Okay. I mean, Easter Sunday is kind of, you know, get to work Sunday, really. This isn't how the story ends. This is . . . this is the next act. But just whilst we're on the Easter Sunday stories, and just to prove I'm not just a kind of a miserable misanthrope, the one detail that I read every Easter Sunday is the encounter in the garden when Mary finds the risen Lord. And he says to her, 'Mary.' That's all he needs to say.

NICK B   Yeah.

NICK S   And that's an extraordinary moment of *personal* understanding. There isn't a description; there isn't a, 'Look, I'm here. Everything's all right.' I call you by name.

NICK B   Yeah.

NICK S   And even now it sends a tingle down my spine, really.

NICK B   Yeah.

NICK S   That's what we are made for; it's to be known by a name that identifies everything we are and the fullness of that relationship. I think that's remarkably powerful detail in the story.

NICK B   That runs through Scripture, you know, particularly for the, for Israel in an exile – where again, you're back to Isaiah 43, for example. You hear this, you know, 'I know you by name.' It's the name all the way through.
        How do you reflect on that?

CHINE I think a lot of my Christian journey, especially in recent years, it feels like it's in Saturday. Which is yes, this, the world is terrible. Something terrible has happened and is constantly happening. And part of what I feel the Christian duty is, is to work towards kind of looking ahead; to imagining the Sunday; to believing that it will happen, despite the realities, despite the fact that it doesn't really ring true; despite the fact that we're like, 'Is God really here?' The world is so terrible. So, I think I am inspired by those Christians who kind of work towards the coming of the kingdom of God. And to play their part in it, rather than just kind of sit passively and not necessarily go to the shops, but do something in that in between. And that is what I find inspiring.

NICK B That's the point, isn't it, that many, many people live in the Saturday of Easter. You know, what I call empty Saturday. Where we have to avoid the temptation to go shopping or to fill it with stuff. Because if we haven't learned to live in that place of emptiness – where we don't know that Sunday's coming, you know, the disciples have been told loads of stuff, but they didn't get it; there wasn't a slot for it in one sense in their brain   and then we can't be surprised by the joy. Or surprised by the bewilderment of Easter Day, unless we've stayed.

It's what an Asian theologian, Kazuki Koyama, talks about in the desert: that when all the significant things that happen in Scripture, happen in deserts. And the thing to do in a desert is not spend your energy in trying to get out of it. Learn to live with it. And someone else once said, the important thing in a desert is to look for the flowers that grow only in the desert. Don't waste your time looking for the flowers that only grow in fertile areas because you're going to miss out big time. So, the Saturday experience is integral to following the Friday and anticipating Sunday.

Thank you very much. That brings us to the end of that conversation. We hope you've enjoyed it. Much more that could have been said, and we hope you'll join us for the third session, which is on being human.

SESSION 3
BEING HUMAN

NICK B   Welcome to the third session of this Advent York Course. The overall theme is *Who am I?* We're looking at what it means to be human, and the theme of this session is really to try and drill down a bit into that. What does it mean to be human?

We've said in previous sessions that our theology has to be earthed. We're a material faith. How do you earth your theology, Nick?

NICK S   That's a very good question and I have difficulty answering it, because my instinctive reaction is, I probably don't, or I don't enough. Because I read a lot, and reading feels like a very sort of *disembodied* experience. You can do it in different places; it doesn't really matter the medium that you're using. It kind of feels a bit weightless, if you see what I mean.

I think that's probably because – I don't really come from *any* Christian tradition; I had no Christian upbringing at all – but the Christian tradition I found myself in was one that was a bit more cerebral and a bit less embodied. Now, the older I've got, the more I have appreciated the physical practices of theology. But I probably don't marry the two enough, as in the physical practice of worship and reading and studying theology.

NICK B   How would you describe theology? Because it sounds, I think, to many people, like it's a bit abstract. It's about, you know, thinking about things.

NICK S   Yeah.

NICK B   How would you describe it?

NICK S   The trite way to describe it is talking about God. That's kind of what it means. But I think it might be better to say telling stories about God. We talked a bit about this in the previous session, about how the Scriptures . . . they're not a philosophical document as such. I mean, in one sense they're not a theological document as such – they're a bunch of stories.

NICK B   Yeah.

NICK S   Letters and laws and poems and so on and so forth. But in one regard, they're very embodied because obviously they were written down at some point in the past, but they're written down by people, who lived at certain times amongst certain communities, who'd experienced certain things, and wanted to narrate certain understandings of God that had emerged through those experiences.

Theology's kind of a continuation of that. It tries in some respects to systematise, and bring some order to those stories and those experiences and those beliefs. And that is necessary. But sometimes you can go too far and you end up with the kind of 'mere' theology, which is dry, desiccated, theorised, and no earthly use to any human being.

CHINE   For me, as someone who studied theology, but . . . studied theology wanting to be a journalist – that was my kind of ultimate aim. I think for me, theology has always . . . I've always asked the question, 'What has this got to do with me?' And 'What's this got to do with the world that I'm living in?' And 'How do I communicate and package this kind of thing that can feel very cerebral or transcendent or difficult to communicate into a way that is digestible?'

And I get to do that a lot with the kind of writing that I do or with the job that I do. We're constantly thinking, okay, well 'What does the Christian story . . . What does our understanding of who God is and who we are as human beings made in the image of God have to say about this thing that is happening in the news today?'

So, for me, that is the earthiness of theology. It can be made relevant to the things that we are experiencing on our TV screens and in our daily lives. And that to me speaks of what incarnation ultimately is. It's God stepping into the human form, but also the human acts, and it's how we can make it accessible and understandable to us as mere human beings.

NICK B   It's one of those difficult things, isn't it? That if you ask, how will the Church be judged? (Church with a big C.)

Well, maybe one answer is, according to Matthew 25, did we visit the poor? Do we look like the Jesus we read about in the gospels? Or do we look like, do we feel like something else? Because if we do, we're a fraud, basically.

CHINE And I think that so often . . . I, guess for us as British people, em . . . the Church has become so much part of our kind of culture and the *grandness* of it and the *ceremony* and the kind of processes and the systems that are kind of engaged with the Christian faith . . . that it can feel difficult to relate that to the Christian story that we read in the New Testament in particular. And you get glimpses of it, with the, kind of, church doing really good things, setting up organisations, setting up food banks, you know? Setting up homeless charities. But actually, on the, kind of, day to day, how do we *model* what we believe the Christian story to be about? And I think, unfortunately, for many people they don't see . . . that is not the story that they hear of the Church. They hear the other stories, or the places in which we have failed. So, I think our responsibility is not just to tell all those good stories, but also to embody the Christian faith ourselves.

NICK S I'll just add an example to this. A number of years ago, BBC Radio 4 had the *You and Yours* phone in; it was talking about debt and mental health. And they had Martin Lewis, who's the money saving expert guy, giving advice. People phoning in, saying some pretty horrendous stories. And it was about the relationship between debt and mental health.

One woman phoned in, and she said her husband had an undiagnosed gambling problem, had racked up £20,000 worth of debt. Couldn't cope anymore. 'Then I answered the phone, then opened letters – they're all debt collections.' She said, 'It's broken us, and it's broken our marriage as well. What should we do?'

And Martin Lewis, um, sponsors very interesting – he's not a Christian at all. I think he's in sympathy with religious groups, but he's not a, you know, he's not an evangelist at all. And he said, 'Well look, you need an organisation that can do two things for you. One, it can get the debts in order, so it can restructure the debts and professionally order your financial situation. But also, an organisation that comes around' – and these were his words – 'holds your hands, makes you a cup of tea, listens to your problems.' *Because* it wasn't just the fact that they had massive financial issues, it's the fact that she said her marriage was falling apart. The organisation he was talking about was CAP, Christians Against Poverty. They were doing theology there.

Because what they're doing is saying, well, there's a problem here. It's a problem of debt, but it's also a relational problem, because you and your relationship with one another has been broken – according to this. So, we're going to do the professional stuff of restructuring the debt with you, but we're going to do the pastoral stuff of being with you, of showing *com*-passion, of suffering alongside you, of walking alongside you.

Now that is theology, really. That is doing the kind of things we do in life every day, but doing them in the way, as it were, smells of God, a bit.

NICK B
Do you think, um, you touched on this I think, Chine, that Christians' failure, you know, the . . . Sometimes Christians are embarrassed about the failings of other Christians, or of the Church as an institution, whichever Church that is. You know, no denomination is exempt from this sort of thing. How do you respond to it, if people say, well, you can write the whole thing off 'cause you lot are a disaster.

CHINE
Well, I think part of what we need to do is recognise that that is the story that people hear, and that is what they understand, and so not try and explain it away. Nor try to separate ourselves from the institution of the Church. So yes, yeah, 'The Church is bad, but I'm all right. I'm a proper Christian. I'm really following Jesus.' I think it's recognising that in all places and all senses that we all fail, and the Church as an institution is, is one of those things that does fail.

Now, what I think is also really important is for us to move beyond those kind of headline stories. For many people, living in local communities, actually they have huge trust in the church that is down the road, whether or not they've ever been into that church. It is a sign of presence and a sign of a place that has open doors, that does stuff, that does God, that smells of God in their community.

So, I think often what we want to do is to draw people away from the kind of big failures to the kind of small acts of love and kindness that they might see and experience in their own communities.

NICK B   Is there any biblical narrative that you would go to in addressing that, Nick?

NICK S   Um, I mean, in one sense, *the* biblical narrative is one of institutional mess up, isn't it? So, I'm tempted to say, all of it!

NICK B   Yeah.

NICK S   I mean, I'm struck by – this is a not an institutional example – Barnabas and Paul, in the New Testament, Acts. Paul's not a guy you want to hang about with, after what he's been doing.

'What are you doing, bringing this lunatic into our midst?' It's a risk-taking thing to do. And if anybody deserves to be shown the door, at this particular stage, presumably it's Paul, because he ain't been an ally.

So, that sort of conjures two sort of thoughts in my mind. One is with regard to institutional failures – yeah, you accuse them. They're morally disgusting. But, if you leave the story at that, you find yourself in a situation, which we find all too often today, which makes me equally unpalatable, which is me effectively passing judgement on a whole load of things in the world that really aren't as good as *me*.

NICK B   Yeah.

NICK S   Well, forget that, okay. 'Cause I know how I would behave in lot those situations. So, it's simultaneously holding this, 'This is morally disgusting; we have forgiveness; we have judgement, and we have second chances.'

NICK B   Isn't part of what it means to be human that we look at the narrative in Scripture and we see that most of the great heroes of the faith are a bit of a disaster. You know, you've got Moses at the beginning, who leads the people out through the Exodus, out of 400 odd years of captivity, having made every excuse in the book. He's a murderer!

NICK S   A murderer, yeah, in the first instance. Yeah.

NICK B   You go right through them. Abraham, great father of the faith, tries to flog his wife off as his sister so the local warlords can have their wicked way with her, and he can save his life. Three times! Not even once! You look at Hebrews 11, the New Testament, the great roll call of the heroes of the faith, and they're all a disaster. I think there's great comfort in this, not in that it justifies us being a disaster when we fail, but it does say, this is the material God works with. To be human, is to begin by recognising mortality and our failure. Every service I go to begins, as an Anglican, with the question, right, 'Who's screwed up?' And we all go, 'We have.' And it's liberating.

NICK S   And it's probably completely inappropriate to quote *In the Thick of It*, the very, the very blue BBC comedy about politics and ten, fifteen years ago. But one of the, one of the characters at one point, one of the SpAds, one of the really aggressive SpAds is listening to a politician who's just complaining about how he's being treated. And the SpAd says – in the cleaned-up version – 'Oh, for goodness sake, stop whining. This isn't *East Enders*. We're all in the same plague pit here.' Well, you're kind of right! We are all in the same plague pit here.

NICK B   Yeah. Yeah. It's what it is to be human.

Well, thank you for being with us for this third session. We hope you've enjoyed it, or, um, maybe it's inspired your curiosity about the biblical narrative and what it means to be a human being or even to be a Christian.

We're going to welcome you back, I hope, to session four, which we've titled 'Playing a Part (not Playing Apart)'.

SESSION 4
PLAYING A PART (NOT PLAYING APART)

NICK B   Welcome to session four of this Advent series for the York Courses, and the theme today – Playing a Part (Not Playing Apart), which I know is a bit corny, but it's really about human agency. It was once said of Pentecost that it was God's invitation to get out of your seat and get onto the stage. This involves us in activity and engagement, not just *spectating* what's going on.

   We live in a very judgemental world, in which I know I'm better than all of those terrible people, 'cause they're terrible. And, it's a way of denying my agency in making the world a better place. What might you have to say? Start with you, Chine, about . . . about human agency, about being a Christian and being an agent of change, rather than simply a spectator of other people's failures?

CHINE   I think part of the beauty of the Christian story and Christian history is the ways in which, inspired by the biblical narrative, people have got involved and they have got out of their seats, and they have done things that have changed their communities and changed their worlds. There is something intrinsic in our faith that makes us active agents, or causes us to be active agents, rather than kind of passive recipients that don't engage in our world.

   I think one of the things I love about the story of Pentecost – one of my favourite passages in all of Scripture – is in Acts 2, where it says, 'When the day of Pentecost came, they were all together in one place'. You think about all those people that were there 'in one place'; they came from different places, they had different theological, political ideas. It would've looked kind of messy and not uniform. And one of the things that I am really inspired by is that *collective* agency as well as the individual – the coming together of people from different backgrounds, from different places, to work together for a particular change. And whatever change that is, whether that's food banks or political, or whether that's, um, sexual abuse, it's kind of that coming together, um despite the difference.

NICK B   Nick?

NICK S   I would agree with all that. I would want to actually import one of the areas of our early discussion to this conversation about agency, which is the gift, an idea I keep on coming back to. Agency is very, very important. Doing stuff *to* people feels great, particularly if you are the do-er.

NICK B   Yeah.

NICK S   Don't get me wrong, it's not bad to do stuff *to* people and *give* them stuff. But much more important, empowering, is the idea of giving them their agency and giving them the capacity, or more accurately, enabling them the capacity to give of themselves. And the experiences that I've seen that in . . . it's *transformative* with people. Because what it says to them is, you are not somebody in need. You're not even just somebody who can choose different options. You are somebody who has something that the world wants. You have something that the world needs. You can contribute. You can give of yourself. And that is so extraordinarily affirming . . . it underlies my underlying point about human beings being made for gift. I think agency is very important, don't get me wrong, but I think there is one step further than agency, which is enabling, empowering, encouraging people to *give* of themselves.

NICK B   There's a great biblical story I always go back to in relation to this, which is Bartimaeus in Mark chapter 10, who is lying at the side of the road when Jesus and his friends come along. Bartimaeus calls out to him. And this is great evangelistic method: Jesus' friends see it as their job to stop him getting close to Jesus. [Everyone laughs.] It's very effective. And the really great thing is that Jesus still hears this man despite the efforts of his friends to keep him away.

But the best bit is that Jesus doesn't go over to Bartimaeus and kneel down, as I might have done, 'And let me show you my best pastoral method here,' you know, 'I've been to college!' Em, he sends the *disciples*, who have just been trying to keep them apart. And they go to him. He says, 'Bring him to me.' They go, and they say, what I think is the best invitation in Scripture: 'Take heart, get up. He is calling you.' Know, 'Take heart . . . You can lie there if you want, but nothing will happen. But if you get up, you take responsibility and he's calling *you*. Not the one behind you, or the one who's got his theology better worked out or anything. He's calling *you*.' It's fantastic invitation.

NICK S It is. And there's another New Testament story that everybody will be familiar with, and I mean everybody, 'cause it's probably the best-known New Testament story. It's the Parable of the Good Samaritan, which I must have read however many times, until I picked up when writing about it a few years ago, that actually there's a very clever twist in the story of the Good Samaritan, I'd never noticed beforehand.

The lawyer says to Jesus, 'Who is my neighbour?' So, the implication there is, 'I am the do-gooder. I want to know *whom* I should be doing good *to*.' Jesus tells the story, and in the end he asks the lawyer, who was the neighbour to the one in need? So the neighbour moves from having been a *passive* recipient of someone else's largesse to an *active*, giving, moral agent themselves. I think that's a really crucial transition.

CHINE I think this feeds into so much of a kind of political understanding of how the world is supposed to be, or how we are supposed to live. There's kind of the idea that we should get stuff, receive stuff, or there's the idea that actually we make our own way in the world, and those things feel in contradiction sometimes.

But actually, one of the things that I've realised, having worked in international development, for example, and communicating international development, is that there is so much more *power* in communicating people living in poverty as people with *agency*. As people with their own sense of worth, identity, family, their own kind of hopes and dreams, rather than kind of just pulling on this idea that we, over here, give of our spare change to them over there, who can't help themselves. So, there is so much more power in that. And we see that in lots of different kind of charity sector communications, is . . . whether it is someone who is living in poverty in an African country, or it is someone, a young person who is in need of employment here . . . if you call them by name, as Jesus does so often in the New Testament, if you say *you matter*, I *care* whether you turn up on time, I *care* whether you do good work and you are someone of agency here. That's so powerful.

NICK B   In one sense, I mean this is an Advent course and Advent is an invitation, if we take the time and the space to ask ourselves the hard questions for when Christmas eventually comes, what sort of Jesus are we looking for? What sort of world is he coming into and what sort of good news does he bring?

How would you begin to, if a 16-year-old stopped you on the street and said, 'Okay, what's it all about, Advent?' What would you say? Put you on the spot, why not?!

CHINE   Funnily enough, I had this, a similar conversation with my 7-year-old last night, who likes to ask theological questions at bedtime – to not go to sleep.

NICK B   Exactly!

CHINE   He was saying, you know, 'Why did God come into this world?' And I said, 'Well, God didn't have a body. So, God needed to kind of step into ourselves to show God's self so that we could see.'

And there is something about, for me, Advent being in the invitation to us to come and see, to come and see the child that has been born; to come and see God looking like us and calling us. So, the invitation is to come and see.

NICK B   Nick?

NICK S   That's a great answer. I want to pick up on actually one word that Chine mentioned there, which Keir, right?, would've been asking, 'Why?' Kids ask that all the time. I mean, kids do not need to be taught to be asked 'Why?'

NICK B   No.

NICK S   Now, I think this is actually a very profound point – that you could put it, philosophically speaking, we are naturally teleological beings. Teleological means concerned about the end. Decades before we ever might use the word teleological, we're asking kids . . . I remember driving with my kids once and one of them looked out the window and said, 'Dad,' said, 'Why is that a car?' [Everyone laughs.] How am I supposed to respond? That question makes no sense. That's the automatic question we ask. I think we are naturally ordered as being towards ends, towards wanting to know why things are happening, but also, as it were, what our ends are. And it strikes me that that might be close to an answer to your question about Advent.

NICK B   Yeah.

NICK S   You know, we are not responsible for what's going on in Ukraine, Gaza, Sudan at the moment. They may weigh very heavily on us, but we're not going to be judged – people sitting around this table, people listening to this – for what's happening there. You can be responsible for, who are you? Why are you? What ends have you been working towards? What goals do you want to achieve? And it seems to me that is both a kind of a legitimate and a realistic question for us to be thinking about and asking at this time. Who am I *intended* to be? And what am I doing – or more accurately not doing – that's *preventing* that from happening?

NICK B   In one sense, the Church . . . the reason for the Church's year, its calendar, is that it takes us together – not individually, but *we together*, you know, not apart, but playing a part in it – it takes us on a journey that is rooted in questions, that as we walk together, a bit like in a previous session we mentioned the couple on the road to Emmaus. No word, Jesus comes alongside them and says, 'What are you talking about?' And they go, 'What's been going on in Jerusalem,' they go. And Jesus says, 'What things?' And he says, 'Are you the only one who doesn't know?' And if I'd been Jesus, I'd go, 'Yeah, of course I do. You know, but . . .'

NICK S   Ta-da! [Everyone laughs]

NICK B   Yeah. He says, I don't want to look thick. Um, then you get that invitation to retell the story, to put it together differently, in a way that then makes sense – is redemptive, whatever language you want to use. And part of the journey through Advent, what gets us to Advent, is that we've celebrated God opting into the world, that *eruption* into the, the world of . . . that we all know, and the earth we tread on and so on . . . We've walked to Calvary and to an empty tomb, which was another beginning, not an ending; it sends us on and we walk through what I call the green period of, you know, normal time, as we learn what Jesus was about, what he said, what he did, and we wrestle with that and we do it together. That's why we go to church. And then, we get towards Advent again, where we go, actually, we're going to have to walk this journey again, and ask what are our expectations of God?

When I expect Christmas to come, what sort of Jesus am I looking for? And am I open to having that corrected or reshaped by the journey and the conversation and the asking of the questions – well, why this and why not that, and how and when and all this sort of stuff. Does that make sense?

CHINE   Yes. And I think about my own Christian journey and how Jesus has looked different to me at different points in my life. And the ways in which Jesus is communicated, illustrated, talked about in different places shapes how we respond, how we act in the world – who we think Jesus is. Do we think Jesus is this triumphant, um, muscly guy as some, um, might think? Or do we think of Jesus as this God who chooses to step into this kind of helpless human form? How beautiful and out of the box that is. So, I think, absolutely, our understanding of who Jesus is, shapes who we are.

NICK B   Nick?

NICK S   This line from T. S. Eliot's *Four Quartets*, which I'm going to misquote, but he says something like, we must wait without hope, for hope would be hope for the wrong thing. So much else that Eliot wrote, there's an enormous profundity in that, we often expect the wrong things and sometimes hope for the wrong things.

Now, waiting without hope, there's different ways of reading that and obviously you need to read it in the context of, of what he's writing. But there is the sense there of waiting with expectation, and waiting in such a way as doesn't have simply a very neatly constructed niche in which, what you hope for is going to fit. Because it don't work that way round. Or the other way round, you fit into his plan rather than he fits into yours.

NICK B   Well, that lies behind, in one sense, *The Life of Brian*, doesn't it? And that narrative in which people expect that freedom, salvation, God coming among them again, they will recognise when they see the Romans booted out. That'll be the evidence that God is among them again. And then what happens? He comes in the most subversive way. And the invitation in Mark chapter 1, to repent, means to look differently for the presence of God in the world as it is, in all the messiness.

NICK S   I mean, you mentioned the, the Emmaus story there and we've talked a little bit about in earlier sessions about resurrection appearances and how, how messy they are. There's another brilliant example of this . . . in one sense, how could they not know?

NICK B   Yeah.

NICK S   It takes a long time. You're journeying with somebody. He asks the question. Their world is being changed, and so it's a slow, progressive, open learning experience.

NICK B	Yeah.
NICK S	But interestingly, one that ends, in that story, with a meal.
NICK B	Hmm.
NICK S	And that's, I think, one thing worth under underlying. We haven't talked about yet, just very briefly, eating food with people is transformative. It totally changes the dynamic you have with them. The sharing physicality of it; it changes conversation; it is a *transformative* experience.
NICK B	Yeah. I think on that note, we draw to a close. But perhaps it makes the point that, as we've done over the last four sessions, this is a journey we go on together, and we have to keep asking the questions, and working it out as we go. 'Cause we change, the world changes, and God cannot be put in a box.
	So, thank you for sharing this course with us. We hope you've enjoyed it. We hope you've found it stimulating, and there'll be another one next year.

NOTES

SESSION 1

1 Bob Abernethy 'Barbara Brown Taylor Profile', PBS: https://www.pbs.org/wnet/religionandethics/2000/05/12/december-1-2000-barbara-brown-taylor-profile/2562/ (accessed 19 December 2024).

2 Fyodor Dostoevsky, *The Brothers Karamazov* (New York, NY: Bantam Classics, 2011), p. 440.

3 C. S. Lewis, *Letters to Malcolm: Chiefly on Prayer* (Glasgow: William Collins, 1964).

4 Martin Luther King, 1963 address to the National Conference of Christians and Jews.

5 Bill Gates' speech at the World Economic Forum, 2008, Davos, Switzerland.

6 Quotation attributed to David Attenborough in the *Sunday Times*.

7 Joan D. Chittister, *Called to Question: A Spiritual Memoir* (Lanham, MD: Sheed & Ward, 2004)

8 'Gods of History' Eric Reeves interviewed by Joel Whitney, https://www.guernicamag.com/gods_of_history/?

9 António Guterres, 'U.N. Refugee Chief: Europe's Response to Mediterranean Crisis Is "Lagging Far Behind"', TIME: https://time.com/3833463/unhcr-antonio-guterres-migration-refugees-europe/ (accessed 19 December 2024).

10 Agatha Christie, *Agatha Christie: An Autobiography* (Glasgow: Collins, 1977), Part X.

11 Martin Rees, *Our Final Century: Will the Human Race Survive the Twenty-first Century?* (London: William Heinemann, 2010).

12 Donald Miller, *A Million Miles in a Thousand Years* (Nashville: Thomas Nelson, 2009).

13 Arthur Miller, *The Collected Essays of Arthur Miller* (London: Bloomsbury Publishing, 2016), p. 232.

14 Aaron Ross, 'Interrogating the NY Times' Anthony Shadid', Mother Jones: https://www.motherjones.com/politics/2012/01/anthony-shadid-libya-syria-house-of-stone/ (accessed 19 December 2024).

15 J. I. Packer and Carolyn Nystrom, *Knowing God Devotional Journal: A One-Year Guide* (Lisle, Il: InterVarsity Press, 2009), p. 20.

SESSION 2

1 Victor Hugo, *The Toilers of the Sea*, trans. Robin Buss (London: Penguin Classics, 2007).

2 Anne Lamott, *Plan B: Further Thoughts on Faith* (London: Penguin, 2006), p. 188.

3 Quotation attributed to Timothy Keller, source unknown.

4 Although this quote is apparently commonly mis-attributed to Harper Lee, there seems to be good evidence that it actually originates from Dr James McCosh (1811–1894), a Scottish philosopher and former president of Princeton University.

5 Quotation attributed to Michael Landon, source unknown.

6 Henri Nouwen, *Discernment: Reading the Signs of Daily Life* (London: SPCK, 2013), p. 129.

7 Charles River Editors, *Antoni Gaudí: The Life and Legacy of the Architect of Catalan Modernism* (Charles Rivers Editors, 2017).

8 Quotation attributed to Rob Bell, source unknown.

9 Timothy Keller, *Every Good Endeavor: Connecting Your Work to God's Work* (London: Penguin Books, 2014).

10 Joyce Meyer, 'Finding your way out of the wilderness', The Layman, 3 October 2013, https://layman.org/finding-way-wilderness/ (accessed 19 December 2024).

11 Ann Voskamp, *One Thousand Gifts: A Dare to Live Fully Right Where You Are* (Grand Rapids, MI: Zondervan, 2011), p. 175.

12 William Sloane Coffin, *A Passion for the Possible: A Message to US Churches* (Louisville, KY: Westminster John Knox Press, 1993).

13 Joni Eareckson Tada, *Anger: Aim it in the right direction* (Carol Stream, IL: Rose Publishing Inc, 2012), p. 12.

14 Frederick Buechner, *Beyond Words: Daily Readings in the ABC's of Faith* (Grand Rapids, MI: Zondervan, 2009), p. 259.

15 Brennan Manning, *The Ragamuffin Gospel: Good News for the Bedraggled, Beat-Up, and Burnt Out* (Sisters, OR: Multnomah Books, 2008), p. 19.

16 Eugene H. Peterson, *A Long Obedience in the Same Direction: Discipleship in an Instant Society* (Lisle, IL: InterVarsity Press, 2012), p. 90.

17 Richard Rohr, *The Art of Letting Go: Living the Wisdom of Saint Francis* (audio CD, Sounds True Inc, 2010).

SESSION 3

1 Nicky Gumbel, @nickygumbel, Twitter/X post 17 April 2014, https://x.com/nickygumbel/status/317362215005073408.

2 Evelyn Underhill, *The Spiritual Life* (1937).

3 Richard Rohr, *Immortal Diamond: The search for our true self* (London: SPCK, 2013), p. 124.

4 Carl Jung, *Psychological Types* (Abingdon: Routledge, 2016), p. 152.

5 Brené Brown, Facebook, 31 March 2018, https://www.facebook.com/brenebrown/posts/heres-what-ive-learned-about-creativity-from-the-world-of-wholehearted-living-an/2025826304099135/ (accessed 19 December 2024).

6 Philip Yancey, *Disappointment with God: Three Questions No One Asks Aloud* (Glasgow: Harper Collins, 2009), p. 39.

7 Reid Belew, 'Shane Claiborne – The Full Interview', *Medium*: https://medium.com/the-badlands/shane-claiborne-the-full-interview-a623c81f6d90 (accessed 19 December 2024).

8 T. S. Eliot, *Shakespeare and the Stoicism of Seneca* (1927).

9 William Barclay, *New Testament Words* (Louisville, KY: Westminster John Knox Press, 2000), p. 23.

10 Dalai Lama, @Dalailama, Twitter/X post, 26 February 2013, https://x.com/DalaiLama/status/306351006231429120?lang=bn (accessed 19 December 2024).

11 Martin Luther King, Jr, ''In a Single Garment of Destiny'': A global vision of justice (Boston, MA: Beacon Press, 2013), p. 75.

12 Dallas Willard, *Living in Christ's Presence: Final words on Heaven and the Kingdom of God* (Downers Grove, IL: Inter Varsity Press, 2014).

13 'Look at Jesus' featuring N.T. Wright, The Work of the People: https://www.theworkofthepeople.com/look-at-jesus (accessed 24 January 2025).

SESSION 4 PLAYING A PART (NOT PLAYING APART)

1 Dallas Willard, 'How Does the Disciple Live?', *Radix Magazine*, Vol. 34.3.

2 David George Moore, 'America, Read this Book!', Patheos: https://www.patheos.com/blogs/jesuscreed/2017/03/25/america-read-book/ (accessed 19 December 2024).

3 Keith Getty, 'Song Story: In Christ Alone', 20 August 2015, *Worship Leader Magazine*: https://worshipleader.com/worship-culture/in-christ-alone/ (accessed 6 January 2025).

4 Evelyn Underhill, *Mixed Pasture: Twelve Essays and Addresses* (Eugene, OR: Wipf and Stock Publishers, 2015), p. 51.

5 Rachel Held Evans, *Searching for Sunday: Loving, Leaving, and Finding the Church* (Nashville, NT: Thomas Nelson Inc, 2015), p. 148.

6 Nancy Pearcey, *Total Truth: Liberating Christianity from its Cultural Captivity* (Wheaton, IL: Crossway, 2008).

7 Mother Teresa, *No Greater Love,* Commemorative Edition (Novato, CA: New World Library, 2016), p. 47.

8 Fleming Rutledge, *Advent: The Once and Future Coming of Jesus Christ* (Grand Rapids, MI: William B. Eerdmans Publishing Co, 2018).

9 Bishop Desmond Tutu https://www.facebook.com/DesmondTutuPF/photos/ christ-like-doesnt-mean-not-having-faults-it-means-that-you-do-actually- have-a-c/1179904575375929/ (accessed 19 December 2024).

10 Bruce Cockburn, 'Cry of a Tiny Babe' lyrics © Warner Chappell Music, Inc.

11 Quotation attributed to William Barclay, source unknown.

12 'If you are what you ought to be, you will set fire to all Italy, and not only yonder.' letter to Stefano Maconi [1376] in *St Catherine of Siena as seen in her letters* tr. Vida D. Soudder (1905). Quoted as 'Be who God meant you to be and you will set the world on fire' by Rowan Williams from the sermon at the wedding of Prince William and Catherine Middleton, Westminster Abbey, 29 April 2011.

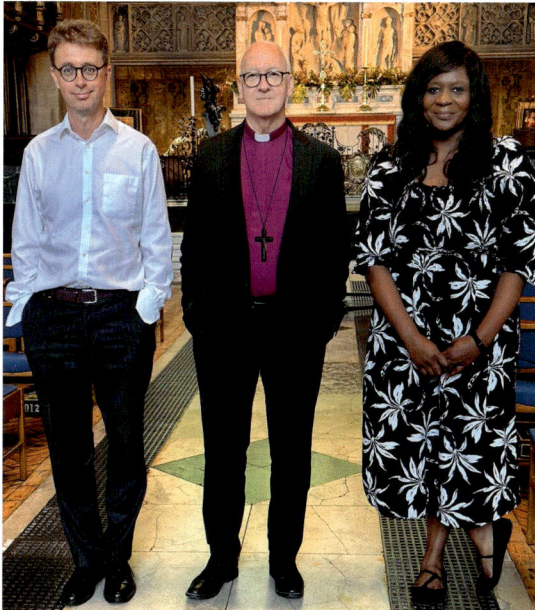

NICK BAINES became the first Bishop of Leeds in June 2014. He was previously Bishop of Bradford and Bishop of Croydon. Before ordination, he worked for four years as a Russian linguist at GCHQ.

Nick has particular expertise in communication and is known for his engagement with the media. He is frequently asked to comment nationally on topical issues, and is regularly heard on *Thought for the Day* on Radio 4. His writing includes comment pieces for broadsheet newspapers, popular books on Christian faith and contributions to academic journals. For nine years he chaired the Sandford St Martin Trust which promotes excellence in religious broadcasting through the presentation of annual awards. Nick became a member of the House of Lords in 2014.

CHINE McDONALD is Director of Theos.

NICK SPENCER is Senior Fellow at Theos.

OUR WARM THANKS to Monkeynut for recording and producing the course audio and video.

York Courses: https://spckpublishing.co.uk/bible-studies-and-group-resources/york-courses